PRAISE FOR JACQUELINE PIRTLE

"Jacqueline takes you always directly to what you are ready to see or experience."

— LONGTIME CLIENT AND READER

"It is liberating to face your own blocks and to be finally free of the weight that they have caused for many years. And while for me the changes I'm experiencing are noticeable and real, I still feel like myself. Just a more sure self."

— LONGTIME CLIENT AND READER

"Jacqueline makes me BELIEVE I can be and live a joyful and magical existence every new day of my life!"

— LONGTIME CLIENT AND READER

JACQUELINE PIRTLE

Align, Expand, and Calibrate!

Your Stairway to Joy

A 90 day journal

THE EXTENDED EDITION

COPYRIGHT

Copyright © 2021 Jacqueline Pirtle
www.FreakyHealer.com

All rights reserved. No part of this book may be reproduced or transmitted in any form or by any means, electronic or mechanical, including photocopying, recording, or by any information storage and retrieval system without the written permission of the publisher, except where permitted by law.

ISBN-13: 978-1-955059-29-9

Publisher: Freaky Healer

Editor-in-chief: Zoe Pirtle
All-round Support: Mitch Pirtle

Book cover design by Kingwood Creations kingwoodcreations.com

Author photo courtesy of Lionel Madiou madious.com

I want to let you know that all my books and work as a holistic practitioner are a wholesome system, supporting you to live a more conscious, mindful, and happier life.

However, I made it so you can receive the benefit of living more joyously solely by working through this terrific journal book, while also experiencing the full satisfaction in continuing on to the next journal of this series—not to mention the rock solid tools you get by reading any of my other books or adding in my podcast *The Daily Freak*. Either way, I know you'll love my inspirational teachings.

Find out more at:
FreakyHealer.com
Amazon - Jacqueline Pirtle's Author Page
The Daily Freak Podcast

Before you dive in, I want to thank you for hopping on the magic train with me! I truly hope you enjoy ***Align, Expand, and Calibrate*** as much as I loved writing it, and if you do, it would be wonderful if you could take a short minute and leave a review on Amazon and Goodreads.com as soon as you can.

Your kind feedback helps other readers find my books more easily, and to be happy faster. Consider it a joy-deed for the world.

Thank you!

ACKNOWLEDGMENTS

Let's be honest here… I have a dream team!

I could not have finished this book without the help of talented, creative, high-for-life, and phenomenal professionals.

From the bottom of my heart, I want to thank Zoe Pirtle for her editorial mastery; Mitch Pirtle for his all-round support; kingwoodcreations.com for their fun and polished book cover design; and madiouART.com for an amazing photo shoot.

I'd also like to extend a huge "Thank You!" to all fans of my work and books—I created this beautiful journal series for you.

Life is spectacular with you on my side!

***Align** yourself with who you really are.*
***Expand** that aligned YOU.*
***Calibrate** into your new height!*

DEDICATION

I dedicate this journal to anyone who feels blahhh - emotionally, physically, or energetically - and with all my might, will pull them into their alignment, expansion, and calibration.

INTRODUCTION

Lovable YOU,

It is, indeed, an intense time that brings forth the values we actually treasure, while also highlighting new ways that keep us going in the long run—or at least until we are shown an even newer version of different. But either way, you are here now, so I hope that you believe in your long-haul.

My heart is filled to the brim to be able to share with you how you can validate your longevity and dive deep into the essence of who you really are, immerse yourself there, and live from that substance filled with energy, wisdom, beauty, and life—becoming unquestionably clear that you are in charge of how - and also what - your quality of existence is and that you can change yourself to being and living more aligned, expanded, and calibrated at any time you wish!

Let's face it:

Without alignment with your deepest inner truth of who you really are, it's easy to feel lost and life can be uncertain. You are missing out on the beauty that you are and what life could be for you.

Without expansion, you are not able to show up as the bigness

INTRODUCTION

that you naturally are—however, if not aligned first, expansion can get you into the direction of unwell-feeling.

Without calibration, you are not being and living the high-for-life energy you came here to BE. But beware, calibrating without aligning only gets you feeling better until whatever - chocolate, cake, or ice cream for instance - that happy-fied you wears off; when calibrating while aligned keeps you shifting higher and higher since there is never a ceiling as to how amazing you can feel. Or take calibration with alignment but no expansion—the steam to get all the way up on your feeling ladder will be little, or missing.

You really, really, really are invited to use the whole system of aligning first, expanding second, and calibrating with joy into the infinite and beyond in order to truly BE and live YOU. I cannot press this point enough!

You might ask, "Is it hard?" No it is not, and anybody who tells you otherwise is wrong, because it's not like you need to learn something new—you already know how to do it and you already ARE all that bliss! All you need is knowledge, practice, and to choose, commit, and focus on a lifestyle that feels amazing —then cultivate it to make it your normal way of existing. Think of it like you are going to the beach in a full body-armor-suit but realize on the spot that it is not fitting or comfortable, so right then and there you plan on wearing a bathing suit next time you go beaching and commit to focus on remembering that more aligned choice you just made—the outcome being that when the day comes and you head to the beach in your bathing suit, you will feel amazing, so much so that you will always put this new custom as a priority since you are now hooked on how incredible it feels.

Alignment, expansion, and calibration shoots you into the sky with the stars; and there - in that open space - a whole world of possibilities, wellness, happiness, and wonder awaits—as well as limitless wisdom that comes from your energetic part - your soul being, your inner you, your higher self, or however you wish to call it - but also from your one-ness with consciousness, where all information is held.

You are a whole being comprised of a physical body, mind, soul, and consciousness, here to experience life through physicality and alignment with your soul being—expanding and calibrating into *bigger* and *more* at all times through human-ness and from the core of the energetic essence that makes everything and everyone. As part of that energetic bundle, you are vibrating in frequencies, some lower than others—preferably higher ones, since they are the frequencies that feel truly amazing. You are capable of switching between these frequencies as you wish. Simply said, what you focus on is how you feel and how you feel creates your next—it's like you are holding a compass and can constantly see where you are, but also where you are headed to:

- I am aligned—feeling great
- I am aligned and expanded—feeling great and powerful
- I am aligned, expanded, and calibrated—feeling great, powerful, and over the moon blissful
- Unaligned, not expanded, not calibrated—without a clue, unwell, and can't stay happy to save your life

This **Align, Expand, and Calibrate** journal exists to help you to BE and live more of YOU and grab this time of intensity with your heart—to shift to feeling amazing anyways, no matter what, by helping you to turn your old ways upside down - and inside out - so the old unconnected way doesn't exist anymore. From there you can find new and unique preferences that fit your aligned being, so you will go out into the world being the bright light that you actually are.

I say, let's not lose another second to any unaligned misery; and instead - as your new aligned, expanded, and calibrated YOU - create a life beyond your dreams where an ocean of opportuni-

INTRODUCTION

ties will catch hold of you, not to mention you will become ONE with joy and gain the excitement of living an extraordinary life filled with incredible manifestations.

Surely you understand that such a lifestyle still includes ups and downs, lefts and rights—lots of great moments for you to practice aligning, expanding, and calibrating. Being okay with however things are - even in hard times - and creating pure alignment by not giving any unaligned thing the oxygen to be the main attraction in your life, means that you are making your aligned, expanded, and calibrated YOU the main star. Just consider the epic-ness of that!

Journaling through this 90 day extended edition of *Align, Expand, and Calibrate* gives your best version of you the spotlight and brings a huge heightening into the equation so you can experience life like you never have before, craft a time beyond your expectations, and love what you live—to the extent of becoming a master in living consciously, mindfully, and feeling phenomenal, while manifesting the best of the best. It's a change that is forever!

As a side note, there are a couple of bonus days at the end in case you ever find the need to do two entries in a day, or so you can keep working while you wait for the next journal in this series to arrive. I also left you a few blank *Align, Expand, and Calibrate* pages to journal about deepening your ways of being proudly alive.

Enough chit-chat, I know you are ready—so grab your pen and have incredible fun catching more life than you have ever caught in your new crazy ways.

Happiest,
    Jacqueline

 Day 1

IMAGINE the most magical and beautiful stairway, one of light and pureness—made of glass, wood, earth, or whatever material is most heart-touching for you. Make this your stairway to joy! Then, visualize your flight of stairs going high up into a space of the infinite, beautiful, and bright nothingness - into consciousness - with the last step meeting the heavens. Sit with this image, stare at it, laugh and cry with it—while filling yourself with its essence of love, light, and holiness. How does this feel for you?

Every split second in life you get to choose to run up those stairs and live in that essence of pure positive energy, or to stay where you are in physicality while only living from that limited space—with yet another option being to only take a few steps up and live half way.

Just think about it—creatively, uniquely, and playfully rushing up your stairway to ecstasy, with every step getting you happier and more inspired to BE and live YOU.

Now that you have created your visionary path of enlightenment we can get into the rootedness of how you take your first step, then - while being endlessly fueled and energized - run up without ever stopping. So be excited—the teachings of alignment, expansion, and calibration are splashed across the next few pages.

_____
_____
_____
_____

Align, Expand, and Calibrate - Your Stairway to Joy

 ay 2

TIME TO FUEL up and energize—time to align!

You are at the bottom of your magical stairway to joy, looking up with excitement and an "I can't wait" attitude, ready to take your first step but also eager to get rushing—for which you need unlimited and powerful fuel that carries you, without any doubt, up and into this infinite field of consciousness.

That is where the alignment with your inner being - your soul being, your higher self, the Divine, or however you would like to call it - comes into the picture because your inner you is pure positive energy, always knows what's best for you, and is the most rock-solid guidance to your bliss; aside from being your immediate and innate connection to the field of consciousness that you are always ONE with. Naturally, aligning with your inner voice will guide you up your stairway while fueling you all the way.

I say, close your eyes and breathe into this purifying fact. Let yourself float around in your nothingness to find your alignment with your everything-ness—your inner you. There, ask yourself, "What is alignment for me, what guidance am I getting, and how does my alignment feel?"

Time to align, align, and align some more!

_____
_____
_____
_____
_____

Align, Expand, and Calibrate - Your Stairway to Joy

ay 3

TODAY WE EXPAND. Like a ballon, but don't worry—you will never ever pop since there is no limit to how much you can expand into being you. No limit; just think about that!

Latching onto yesterday's wisdom of aligning with who you really are - a well-feeling energetic being here to experience physical life - it's time to get bigger as that ecstatic YOU.

Imagine your grandness - your pure positive energy - getting bigger, bigger, and bigger—filling every single cell of yours, then growing beyond yourself, even bigger and bigger, until you are flowing into the outer-world and even there getting bigger and bigger to reach beyond and all the way into the infinite.

You are expanding your wholesome YOU; your aligned power, knowledge, connectedness, and incredibly bright light to BE and live as ONE with, in, and through the nothingness of the Universe.

How does that feel—to BE and live that aligned and expanded YOU?

_____
_____
_____
_____
_____
_____
_____
_____
_____
_____

Align, Expand, and Calibrate - Your Stairway to Joy

 ay 4

CALIBRATE YOURSELF INTO A HIGHER, purer, and brighter essence to BE and live as the highest YOU in the most heightened event of all time—your life!

Why? Because for one, you can, and two, how else could you possibly want to live aside from experiencing the whole life-show fully? Lastly, three: life and you are an ongoing development, so keep up with that skyrocketing way of being because there is never a ceiling to how calibrated you can feel.

It's like you are climbing your stairway to joy, bliss, happiness, health, success, abundance, and all that you want to BE and have —always higher and higher while never stopping or going back down, knowing that higher and purer is your calling and that living life is an opportunity to immerse yourself into more and more well feeling.

How does this feel—what are your thoughts here? How will you take that next step to calibrate yourself into your new height?

_____
_____
_____
_____
_____
_____
_____
_____
_____

Align, Expand, and Calibrate - Your Stairway to Joy

ay 5

QUESTIONS OF THE DAY:

Are you aligned? Are you expanded? Are you calibrated—and do you keep aligning, expanding, and calibrating? Are you aligned with who you really are? Are you expanded as such? Are you calibrated into whatever life is for you right now?

Sit for a minute, close your eyes, and breathe into your inner space—potentize yourself! From there, imagine and sense yourself taking these uplifting steps and ascending your magical stairway.

How do you feel? How does everything look in this new height—how does it smell and taste up there, what new thoughts do you have?

Embrace your new day by being and living in that higher essence that you are, and constantly moving into. Wow, what an elevation—be prepared, wonder awaits!

___

Align, Expand, and Calibrate - Your Stairway to Joy

 ay 6

Issues, problems, drama, trouble, difficulties, hardships, and all other unwanted things that life readily offers at times are normal and not there for us to hate, or to wish they would disappear—instead, they exist to be embraced and for you to align with, expand in, and calibrate yourself to new plateaus where change is possible. So be OK with what IS, lean into everything, align with what it means, expand as that wiser you, and calibrate upward; taking the next steps on your stairway of bliss. Remember, your flight of stairs is always there and ready—no matter the circumstances.

What in your life is such a grand event that it just does not move or shift, despite your hard work? How can you align, expand, and calibrate in it?

_____
_____
_____
_____
_____
_____
_____
_____
_____
_____
_____
_____
_____

Align, Expand, and Calibrate - Your Stairway to Joy

 Day 7

YESTERDAY WE COVERED the unwanted that you can't change—today we tap into the unwanted that is, in fact, changeable by you.

What is in your life that you don't like, but could shift with a little more positiveness, a drop of joy, some laughter, or more play? Where could showing up as a more aligned, expanded, and calibrated YOU fit the bill? Where could you give a lot less momentum to the unwanted, and instead, focus straightforward on what you like or the outcome that you are wishing for?

Align, Expand, and Calibrate - Your Stairway to Joy

ay 8

WHEN YOU ENJOY something - be it food, music, or anything really - it means that you are aligned, not just with your inner being but also with what you are enjoying. That's double the win! What in your new day will you make sure to enjoy more consciously? How will you focus on the many alignments in that satisfaction—and how can you make more of this sweetness come to fruition?

_____
_____
_____
_____
_____
_____
_____
_____
_____
_____
_____
_____
_____
_____
_____
_____
_____
_____
_____
_____

Align, Expand, and Calibrate - Your Stairway to Joy

ay 9

YOU CHANGE—PHYSICALITY always changes, and life is constantly new and different with every split second there is. That's just how it works. Naturally, that brings into the equation the fact that your alignment with your inner you and who you really are is also of a changing nature—hence yesterday *this* felt great, but today something else would feel better. What an excitement that brings! You want to move with that thrill so keep yourself on your tippy toes and stay alert by aligning with this always-newness of yourself and life at all times. What is not feeling good for you right now—and what new alignment is possible?

_____
_____
_____
_____
_____
_____
_____
_____
_____
_____
_____
_____
_____
_____
_____
_____

Align, Expand, and Calibrate - Your Stairway to Joy

 ay 10

CLOSE YOUR EYES and take a nice big breath in while sensing yourself - energetically and physically - expanding more and more. Then, while breathing out, settle your expanded YOU by imagining yourself grounding deep down into Mother Earth—drilling yourself in a rooted matter into her core of love and nourishment. Again, breathe in and expand, and keep drilling while breathing out. Do this visualization, this sensing, for as long as you like and on you go into your new day—expanded and substantially powerful, as being the energy that you really are. Wow!

___
___
___
___
___
___
___
___
___
___
___
___
___
___
___
___
___

Align, Expand, and Calibrate - Your Stairway to Joy

 ay 11

ALIGNING IS like a superpower that is naturally always available for you to use and, once trained, you ARE - and stay - aligned without even focusing on it. But here's the catch; you can align with *this* or *that*, with what's good for you or what gets you into your personal abyss—maybe even someone else's "down" if you happen to latch onto theirs. So let's practice aligning with your bliss by focusing on what makes you feel amazing, all while noticing when you're aligning with the opposite. Are you feeling good right now and are you consciously aligning with that joy? Or are you not feeling good—and if so, what can you do about it?

_____
_____
_____
_____
_____
_____
_____
_____
_____
_____
_____
_____
_____
_____
_____
_____

Align, Expand, and Calibrate - Your Stairway to Joy

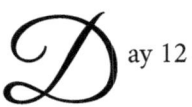 ay 12

YESTERDAY WE SET the record straight for well-feeling and focused alignment, so let's add a little more to that...

Watchful, observant, and concentrated alignment means that you don't indulge in anything that is the opposite—no gossiping, no re-telling of the unwell, no sharing or wreaking havoc, and no feeding or nourishing anything that dims your light—or someone else's. How will you refrain from any of the above from now on?

Align, Expand, and Calibrate - Your Stairway to Joy

ay 13

WHAT ALIGNED food are you dreaming of? Yes, there is such a thing as aligned food! How can you make this meal-magic happen? How will you expand in that enjoyment, calibrating into your highest joyful self while devouring the magic—maybe even sharing and spreading your bliss with a loud "Mmm..." or "Wow?" Can you include your loved ones in this delicious food-play?

_____
_____
_____
_____
_____
_____
_____
_____
_____
_____
_____
_____
_____
_____
_____
_____
_____
_____
_____
_____

Align, Expand, and Calibrate - Your Stairway to Joy

 ay 14

SOME DAYS it's best to hang around like a sloth, slow and lazy in a happy fashion. At other times, it is best to be a dolphin—playful, swift, and adventurous while moving powerfully and with the flow. There is also the feel of being a giraffe—seeing and experiencing everything from a birds-eye view. You change all the time, and so does your aligned physical activity level and way of being. What is best for you right now? Go on, keep up by aligning with your newness—one in which you can expand and calibrate to become a better feeling you.

___
___
___
___
___
___
___
___
___
___
___
___
___
___
___
___
___
___

Align, Expand, and Calibrate - Your Stairway to Joy

ay 15

ALIGNMENT IS EVERYWHERE! The sidewalk shows you where to walk; how aligned! When driving, the lines show you how to stay in place—and in perfect alignment. Cooking with a recipe tells you all about alignment. When putting on pants, your legs give you the aligned direction. Alignment is all around you! Where can you notice it more, and how will you feel yourself - and expand and calibrate - into those great reminders?

_____
_____
_____
_____
_____
_____
_____
_____
_____
_____
_____
_____
_____
_____
_____
_____
_____
_____
_____
_____

Align, Expand, and Calibrate - Your Stairway to Joy

 ay 16

EXPANSION—YOU see it in hairbands, stretchy toys like *Monkey Noodles,* or any kind of dough—even play dough. Where in your surroundings do you notice expansion right now? Why not latch onto these possibilities of expansions that are, in truth, great invitations to feel yourself expanded at all times? Could getting yourself some stretchy slime be your constant reminder?

Align, Expand, and Calibrate - Your Stairway to Joy

 ay 17

PHYSICAL EXPANSION IS JUST as important as energetic expansion. Stretching while doing exercise is a great way to practice and stay physically expanded, and since exercise is good for you, you are naturally aligned - that is, if you are enjoying your chosen fitness type - while also expanding in that wonderful alignment. Are you enjoying your physical activity—and if not, what's a good change? How will you move yourself into your well-feeling physical expansion more often and how can you make this widening count on your conscious level?

_____
_____
_____
_____
_____
_____
_____
_____
_____
_____
_____
_____
_____
_____
_____
_____
_____

Align, Expand, and Calibrate - Your Stairway to Joy

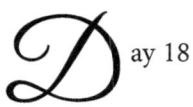 ay 18

ENERGETIC EXPANSION IS ACHIEVED by meditation, visualization, and imagination—then by sensing your energy as expanded. If you can tell the world to go away right now, do it, and get practicing to make this your normal and automatic way of being and living! If not, you can always set your expectation to "I AM expanded!" by breathing into the sensation of being wide, tall, stretching far, and by saying, thinking, or writing the words, "I AM always expanded!" Since this is just one of many mantra-ideas, what is the most fitting one that you can come up with; one that snaps you automatically into being the infinite energetic YOU that you naturally always ARE?

Align, Expand, and Calibrate - Your Stairway to Joy

Day 19

THIS ONE IS EASY—COME up with your best ever mantra for snapping you out of your mis-alignment—and gets you with speed back into alignment? It could be as simple as, "I AM always aligned!" but I'm sure you can unique-fy that statement a thousand times more fitting for yourself. Go on, no holding back here, and keep returning to add more as you go!

___

Align, Expand, and Calibrate - Your Stairway to Joy

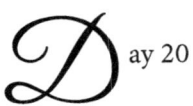 ay 20

ANOTHER MANTRA—ANOTHER chance of getting to know yourself better and better!

What is your shout-out for immediate calibration into the highest you that you are invited to BE and live? Keep this journal entry going - like a tab - by adding on while you live your beautiful life.

_____
_____
_____
_____
_____
_____
_____
_____
_____
_____
_____
_____
_____
_____
_____
_____
_____
_____
_____
_____
_____
_____

Align, Expand, and Calibrate - Your Stairway to Joy

 ay 21

EXPANSION ON A SOUL-LEVEL!

What does that look like for you? What insights does this bring—wisdom of more connectedness, being even more powerful and brighter than before; healthier, happier, or more abundance?

Your soul is always limitlessly expanded and invites you to play catch-up in every new split second that you are alive. How will you play the best ever gotcha-game with your inner YOU?

___

Align, Expand, and Calibrate - Your Stairway to Joy

 ay 22

AN EXPANDED mind thinks expanded thoughts—musings like being open, allowing, receiving, and interested in new ways to experience life are of such a nature. How will you focus on expanding your mind more often? How will you let your old habits go and, instead, choose new exciting ones? Life is colorful, full of differences, and no one way is perfect. I say, give the unpredictable magic a go!

Align, Expand, and Calibrate - Your Stairway to Joy

 Day 23

CHALLENGE TIME!

Set a timer to give yourself a goal to get into alignment - like 5 minutes or so - then go do whatever it takes for you to feel connected and flowing with your inner being and well-feeling. Dance, breathe, smile, or juggle—see if you can succeed!

This helps you strengthen your joy-muscles to make your life the best it can be while also, as a game, creating incredibly potent alignment, expansion, and calibration.

Involve your loved ones - especially kids - and be ready, because giggles are about to become your new normal.

Align, Expand, and Calibrate - Your Stairway to Joy

 ay 24

ALIGNMENT in and with your positive mind is key to living a wonderful life, because what you think you will feel, and that mix together creates your next—which explains why you want to align with good feeling thoughts, even though lots of times it's easier to go for the negative since most of us are well trained in the downer-thought compartment.

But you actually have power! Your conscious focus can shift any thought to positive by choosing better beliefs more and more, programming you to automatically BE and live in a new high-for-life and better way!

How will you accomplish that? Is it by making a positive-thought list, finding the well-feeling opposite of every unwell thought, or by going with your gut that is saying, "What you just thought doesn't feel good, please choose better?"

_____
_____
_____
_____
_____
_____
_____
_____
_____
_____
_____
_____

Align, Expand, and Calibrate - Your Stairway to Joy

Day 25

ALIGNING with good feelings that help you to enjoy life is a choice—maybe not one that feels natural, but one that can be learned.

Focus like a hawk on your feelings. Notice when you don't feel good, and do something about it—best to do so with urgency! How will you make sure that you will give all your might?

Align, Expand, and Calibrate - Your Stairway to Joy

 ay 26

EXPANDING in all well-feelings is a natural remedy for longevity—turning up your joy and vividness and re-setting every cell of your whole being towards healing, success, and abundance, which is in direct alignment with your inner soul-you. So instead of being happy and immediately brushing it off to go on to the next adventure, pause when you feel phenomenal and breathe into expanding yourself wide and big in that beautiful essence—the same way you spread yourself wide on your comfy sofa. Go overboard here, remember; it's a winning thing to do!

Align, Expand, and Calibrate - Your Stairway to Joy

 ay 27

CALIBRATING IS an action that can be done on many levels. Energetically, it means that you are right there side-by-side with your ever-calibrated soul being. Why? Because your inner being is always in THE capacity of height at any given moment, one that - of course - always changes and shifts. How will you stay on top of this energetically exhilarating way of living? Be ready, tomorrow we talk physical calibration!

Align, Expand, and Calibrate - Your Stairway to Joy

 Day 28

CALIBRATING on your physical level means that you live life vividly with your physical body—of course, to whatever extent is healthy and enjoyable for you. Why? When you are physically strong, you naturally feel powerful and that is in direct alignment with your impressive inner being—and expanding as such is invaluable. Are you pushing yourself to a good limit, or could you go a bit further with your physical body? What's possible for you?

_____
_____
_____
_____
_____
_____
_____
_____
_____
_____
_____
_____
_____
_____
_____
_____
_____

Align, Expand, and Calibrate - Your Stairway to Joy

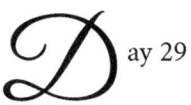 ay 29

CALIBRATING the *action of thinking* into the frequency of a winner mind is…

You guessed it, thrillingly successful!

What calibrated thoughts can you come up with? Which ones will you choose to think all the time and pick over all else, to guarantee limitless enjoyment in your day-to-day moments?

_____
_____
_____
_____
_____
_____
_____
_____
_____
_____
_____
_____
_____
_____
_____
_____
_____
_____
_____

Align, Expand, and Calibrate - Your Stairway to Joy

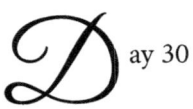# Day 30

CAN you align with joy today, tomorrow, and ever after? Can you expand in the essence of bliss right now? Can you calibrate to BE and live as the biggest most powerful happiness—and is *pronto* possible? Great, so get on it! Now, even better—can you make this way of being and living your normal everyday style?

Align, Expand, and Calibrate - Your Stairway to Joy

 ay 31

WHAT ARE aligned words for you? Are they along the lines of happiness, yumminess, peace, rest, fun, love? What about aligned actions, activities, or happenings? List please!

___

Align, Expand, and Calibrate - Your Stairway to Joy

 Day 32

WHAT WORDS RESONATE with the meaning of *expansion* for you? Stretching, wiggling, or being like the horizon—would any of these fit the bill? What about expanded actions and activities? List please!

___

Align, Expand, and Calibrate - Your Stairway to Joy

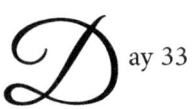 ay 33

WHAT CALIBRATED phrases or words can you come up with? How about: Glimmering like a gem, dancing with the stars, giggling with rainbows? What about calibrated activities and actions? List please!

___

Align, Expand, and Calibrate - Your Stairway to Joy

 ay 34

WHAT WOULD it take for you to align, expand, and calibrate into the essence of worth and value? I'm talking about self-worth and self-value, but also money and all other forms of abundance. How will you get into the deliciousness of tasting, smelling, seeing, and feeling yourself and life as such abundance?

Align, Expand, and Calibrate - Your Stairway to Joy

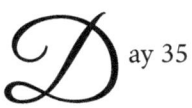 Day 35

How can you get yourself in alignment with perfect health, and with the meaning that health - physical, energetical, emotional, and mindful - carries for you? What will you do to expand in this amazing frequency, and how will you calibrate as that all-over-healthy-you more often?

___

Align, Expand, and Calibrate - Your Stairway to Joy

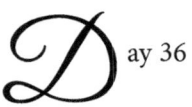 Day 36

Your heart shows you the way unmistakably clear because your ever-knowing soul being lives in your heart, so naturally following that wisdom will get you exactly where you want to be. How can you align with the nudges of your heart on a more trusting level? How can you expand with that knowledge in a deeper way, and how can you calibrate together with your huge heart and the massive love it produces more often? Go on, don't be shy!

Align, Expand, and Calibrate - Your Stairway to Joy

 Day 37

WHAT DO YOU WANT? When do you want it? Why do you want it? And best of all, how do you make it happen?

Align with your what, when, why, and how—then expand to BE and live in the desired frequency while calibrating to match what it is that you are dreaming of. Make your wish-list!

___

Align, Expand, and Calibrate - Your Stairway to Joy

 ay 38

THERE IS ALWAYS a negative and a positive.

Take a sweet treat; it can be enjoyed or worried over because of weight and health.

Look at money—it can be seen as abundance but also as a curse.

Have a burst pipe? It can be good - getting a new pipe - or bad —because you need to fix it.

Every job has a good and a not so good part.

Even every health emergency can be perceived as either a gift in disguise, or a misfortunate experience.

Everything always has two sides—or two ends if you will! How can you align with the more positive perspective of everything by leaving the negative out of your experience? This really matters, so be persistent!

_____
_____
_____
_____
_____
_____
_____
_____
_____
_____
_____
_____
_____

Align, Expand, and Calibrate - Your Stairway to Joy

 Day 39

WONDERING about what's wrong never gets you to what's right! So why do you think you are spending so much focused time and energy on what you think is wrong? You guessed it, it's your old recordings and very well practiced habits that keep you in their grip. I say, "The heck with it," because you are in charge and have the power to declare, "Enough!"

How will you align with all that's right, wonderful, amazing, and that feels good with more attention?

Expand right there and calibrate into a height where you can not only see the stars, but also touch them!

Align, Expand, and Calibrate - Your Stairway to Joy

# Day 40

ALIGNING NEVER MEANS that you are giving up or giving in—even when you choose to turn away or go with how things already are. Aligning always means that you are straightforward with yourself so you are truly YOU—claiming your power and taking charge so you can BE and live strong and control your focus, feelings, thoughts, and views, while creating your life.

Power without control is destructive, however, power that is controlled can move worlds—not to mention that if you expand and calibrate as such, you have THE mightyness on your side.

Align, Expand, and Calibrate - Your Stairway to Joy

 ay 41

AN EXPANSION TAKES place anytime you say *YES* to yourself, to who you really are, and to what you want to BE and live as. Just think of it! The word *YES* carries the energetic value of opening, allowing, and freely receiving—a truly expanded essence. Knowing that, how many times can you say "Yes!" today and every day after?

Great examples are: "Yes" to life, health, happiness, abundance, and yourself, while also to others and how they are living their truth, because the best expansion happens when you start saying yes—regardless of the temptation to say no.

_____
_____
_____
_____
_____
_____
_____
_____
_____
_____
_____
_____
_____
_____
_____
_____

Align, Expand, and Calibrate - Your Stairway to Joy

 ay 42

EVERY FEELING IS a calibration taking you deeper into your inner gold, even if the feeling is sadness, anger, or frustration—that is, if you are not getting caught up in its drama but in its beauty. Why? Because every single feeling is part of you and pure wisdom, an offering coming from your inner you—always yours to feel, heal, and if needed, to let go.

What feeling-calibration can you start to accept, respect, appreciate, thank, and even love newly? Which ones are worthy of your highest celebration through sensing the height they truly are?

_____
_____
_____
_____
_____
_____
_____
_____
_____
_____
_____
_____
_____
_____
_____
_____
_____

Align, Expand, and Calibrate - Your Stairway to Joy

 Day 43

TEMPTATIONS ARE magical invitations - but only if aligned with your inner light - for you to expand and calibrate into your next itch by taking their calls fully and vividly—because after all, every experience is a stepping stone for the next, and the next, and the next to come. What aligned temptations are there for you right now? Are you holding back, and if so, why? Of course, I am always only talking about the well-feeling ones.

___

Align, Expand, and Calibrate - Your Stairway to Joy

Day 44

TO BE and live YOU is only hard if you are going against your alignment, or if you are not listening to the guidance of your perfect alignment. Some difficulties also come from staying stagnant, or stuck, in that alignment without ever giving yourself the permission to also expand as such—because deep down you know that there is more to living your life. Not to mention that staying on the same level without ever calibrating higher can cause roadblocks or stagnancy. You see dear one, you are meant for bigger things - all the time - and I am here to highlight for you to step into what's yours with infinite exuberance.

_____
_____
_____
_____
_____
_____
_____
_____
_____
_____
_____
_____
_____
_____
_____
_____

Align, Expand, and Calibrate - Your Stairway to Joy

 Day 45

WHEN WILL you give up the fight, the resistance and pushing against, the hard work, and the keep-trying-to-make-it-happen, when your alignment clearly states that whatever you are trying so hard to make happen is not for you, wants to happen naturally, or to happen in a different way? Can I get you to stop and breathe—and ask what your true alignment in this fiasco would be? You might be surprised how relieved you will feel, and how easily and swiftly the fitting will happen.

_____
_____
_____
_____
_____
_____
_____
_____
_____
_____
_____
_____
_____
_____
_____
_____
_____
_____
_____

Align, Expand, and Calibrate - Your Stairway to Joy

 Day 46

IN ORDER TO deeply and truly align, expand, and calibrate, you need time well spent alone, quiet, and available to sit still without any agenda whatsoever. Fill yourself with that beauty because that essence is the equivalence of the inner pure positive energetic you. Are you ready for that much bliss? How will you make it happen, and not be too busy or forget?

_____
_____
_____
_____
_____
_____
_____
_____
_____
_____
_____
_____
_____
_____
_____
_____
_____
_____
_____
_____

Align, Expand, and Calibrate - Your Stairway to Joy

 ay 47

WHEN WAS the last time you checked in with yourself to ask, "How am I doing and feeling?" "Am I enjoying?" "Am I aligned with my bright light?" "Am I expanded in my magic?" "Am I calibrated to my maximum height that is possible for me right now?" This also goes for asking yourself things like; "When was the last time I danced, laughed, giggled, joked, crafted, colored, played, and did nonsense stuff?" Go on, be an honest bee here!

___

Align, Expand, and Calibrate - Your Stairway to Joy

 ay 48

WHAT'S BETTER than feeling phenomenal? Nothing!

Why? Because when you feel that thrilled you are totally aligned with your inner being, expanded in the most humongous way, and calibrated all the way high up into the heavens. So take note of that!

Are you feeling that incredible right now? If yes, keep rocking this suiting style. If not, what could you do to shift yourself ASAP?

Align, Expand, and Calibrate - Your Stairway to Joy

 Day 49

A FISH TRYING to be a frog would be called unaligned—whereas a fish trying to be a fish is very fittingly aligned.

Are you trying to be you, or are you choosing to fit something else?

This is such a simple yet elaborately rich in wisdom journal entry. How *can* you make sure to be more YOU—and how *will* you make sure of it? What's the feeling you are gunning for in such a YOU-aligned state?

___

Align, Expand, and Calibrate - Your Stairway to Joy

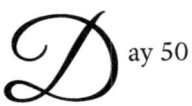 ay 50

WHEN YOU LOOK up into the sky, you can see how every thing naturally is always aligned with itself and each other - for example, the sun is aligned with itself and with the moon and stars in the expanded essence called space - not to mention how highly calibrated all of these wonders are up there. Do you sense the automation and the "of course it's like that" this represents?

That is the alignment, expansion, and calibration we are talking about; *that* is the natural state you want to achieve, like it's the most normal thing ever. Because, after all, it IS!

Align, Expand, and Calibrate - Your Stairway to Joy

 ay 51

Do you feel like you are at your highest level of feeling well—one that goes beyond your imagination of being? Could you go even higher and more amazing? Of course you can, since there is never a ceiling as to how high you could feel—not to mention that you are a changing energy at all times! How will you take this challenge, leading you into your newfound height?

___

Align, Expand, and Calibrate - Your Stairway to Joy

Day 52

Is a body with symptoms of pain, discomfort, and such aligned, expanded, and calibrated? That depends; because a symptom is born out of dis-alignment, but the wisdom it brings is in alignment, and when you listen to the message the outcome is alignment. As for expansion, your symptom's level of intensity shows you how expanded into the direction of dis-alignment you are—but when healing sets in, your expansion shifts towards alignment. Lastly, a symptom calibrating you downward - so you feel yucky - exposes how much higher you could BE and live by aligning, which in exchange shoots you directly into your calibrated state in any given situation.

So it really all depends on how you deal with your physical ailments, but one thing is for sure—it is never too late to react in a wise way because you can always turn anything around and be aligned, expanded, and calibrated ASAP. I say, don't wait!

_____
_____
_____
_____
_____
_____
_____
_____
_____
_____

Align, Expand, and Calibrate - Your Stairway to Joy

 ay 53

THE ALIGNMENT that we are focusing on in this journal is your connection to your inner being—which is the biggest part of you, is filled with infinite wisdom, always loves and guides you to the best outcome, and never ceases to exist since it is energetic and eternal. How would you describe your relationship with that being right now? How do you wish this companionship would be, and what could you do to fulfill this magical life-ship from your end? Making room for you to BE and live yourself truly but also making time to hang out is definitely a priority—but what, and how, else could you carry this out?

Align, Expand, and Calibrate - Your Stairway to Joy

 ay 54

TOMORROW, next week, later, or when *this* or *that* happens...

What a convenient and well trained way to live life, as well as easier and peasier right at the actual moment—but then comes the aftermath of not changing anything, not evolving in a fitting direction, and not getting better, happier, or - as some might say - luckier.

So, what are you putting off? Is it good to wait, and if so, why do your reasons to wait feel good? If holding your horses is not fitting, how can you start racing for a shift?

Get to the bottom of your waiting game and make sure it is aligned. If aligned, keep waiting - tomorrow we talk about those good keep-it-on-hold reasons - and if not go for what's aligned, what feels good—because fear, distrust, disbelief, or other downer habits are currently running your show.

Align, Expand, and Calibrate - Your Stairway to Joy

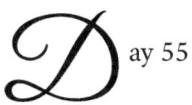 Day 55

WAITING it out can be very beneficial, but only if that stagnant state is aligned - as covered yesterday - and you are expanded in that peaceful space of "I'd love to wait on this one" or "I gave it to the Universe, so let's see what happens."

In those life situations, calibrate into the power of knowing that you have divine help and are always co-creating with the Universe; that things always work out for you, and that life loves you immensely. Then, lightfully enjoy your height!

Align, Expand, and Calibrate - Your Stairway to Joy

 ay 56

How would your aligned world look and how do you see, feel, behave, act, taste, smell, and think there in that magic? How ARE you in it—happy, balanced, wishful, and full of zest? Create your beneficial world here, then visualize and sense the shift you are creating for yourself.

___

Align, Expand, and Calibrate - Your Stairway to Joy

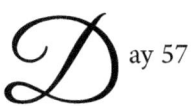 Day 57

How would your expanded world look—and how ARE you in this open wonderland? Is it easy for you to feel, BE, and live, expanded, being in such a wide environment? Make your case, then get your bottom into living it for real!

Align, Expand, and Calibrate - Your Stairway to Joy

 Day 58

How would your calibrated world look? You know, one that is high-for-life no matter the ups and downs and lefts and rights in life. Close your eyes and breathe into this vision, feel the excitement and beyond that this environment carries. Go highest here —make it your reality!

Align, Expand, and Calibrate - Your Stairway to Joy

 ay 59

WHAT IS beauty and beautiful to or for you—not just on a visionary plateau but also on your feeling, tasting, smelling, acting, behaving, thinking, and living level?

Describe in detail what gorgeousness represents for you, then take a minute and realize the wonderful shift you just created. Breathe into this bliss!

Go into your new day aligned with your own personal beauty-meaning, because that will serve you with even more of that pleasing energy—besides, this feeling-state is a pure connection to your inner you made of the essence of beauty.

_____
_____
_____
_____
_____
_____
_____
_____
_____
_____
_____
_____
_____
_____
_____
_____

Align, Expand, and Calibrate - Your Stairway to Joy

 ay 60

You and cream cheese have it all figured out!

Think how creamy and smoothly it spreads—how willingly and without creating roadblocks - chunks - it expands.

You, being made of energy, can do the same because energy has the capability and desire to spread and widen without ever having limits, pressure, resistance, or going against this gift of being able to widen freely.

How will you be your unique spread today, tomorrow, forever and ever—and expand to your aligned liking and well-feeling?

_____
_____
_____
_____
_____
_____
_____
_____
_____
_____
_____
_____
_____
_____
_____
_____
_____
_____

Align, Expand, and Calibrate - Your Stairway to Joy

Day 61

IN ORDER for a plant or tree to thrive and grow it needs dirt, water, and sunshine—that environment IS its alignment to expand as a plant or tree and calibrate into more growth.

It's no different for you! You need your aligned puzzle-pieces to be in place so you can advance in your you-ness.

What are your needs; what is crucial for you, what do you want? Create your aligned list and go make it happen so you can expand and calibrate higher and higher.

Align, Expand, and Calibrate - Your Stairway to Joy

# Day 62

TO SHOW YOU THAT ALIGNING, expanding, and calibrating is normal and your birthright, here is a great visual:

Imagine a bird on the ground. It aligns with its superpower of being able to fly; next, it expands its wings so it can fly. Then, it calibrates higher to get off the ground. Without these steps, it would fail, and probably be really unhappy and unsatisfied since it's not living what it came here to BE and live as.

That scenario is witnessed all the time and seen as "this is how it is," and "it's all normal and natural."

What's keeping you from doing the same, as your human you? How will you step into what you are capable of being and living?

Align, Expand, and Calibrate - Your Stairway to Joy

Day 63

PICK something that you are really picky about—it can be food, clothes, lifestyle, cleanliness of your home, your feelings, decorations, different moods, your passion, or even your work. Important: you have to be fussy about how this chosen thing needs to be in order for you to feel good about it, there is no leeway for anything to be different.

Realize that you are actually very aligned with what feels good and whatnot in this exercise; notice that you are very strongly expanded as that aligned you, and sense the powerful calibration you ARE in that has-to-be-like-that pickiness.

Where in your life can you apply this absolute must-be-like-that more often? Maybe in your happiness, joy, and bliss department? Make all of them a must!

_____
_____
_____
_____
_____
_____
_____
_____
_____
_____
_____
_____
_____
_____

Align, Expand, and Calibrate - Your Stairway to Joy

 Day 64

IN ORDER TO have money you must align with the essence of money—the value of abundance, goodness, freedom, without a care in the world, and being able to share and spread it limitlessly, making others feel amazing too.

So, be aware of unhelpful old recordings about money! Of it being evil, hard to get, never enough, even undeserving—instead, align with its magic, expand in its beauty, and calibrate as the bundle of light it really is by climbing higher and higher with its energetic value, but also your own essence of worth.

How will you get into this bliss more often? Would meditating, opening your heart, and seeing abundance everywhere - in you and around you - work?

___
___
___
___
___
___
___
___
___
___
___
___
___
___

Align, Expand, and Calibrate - Your Stairway to Joy

ay 65

ONE ALIGNED PERSON is always more powerful and inspirational than a million unaligned *blahhh* people! Why? In alignment sits your power, because there you are connected to your rock-solid and always knowing inner being, your backbone. Add to that alignment your expansion and calibration as such, and you have the most potent, dynamic, wide-open, and highest being ever. I know that's you—because hey, you are working through this journal. Question is, are you showing up as such every day—or even better, at all times?

___
___
___
___
___
___
___
___
___
___
___
___
___
___
___
___

Align, Expand, and Calibrate - Your Stairway to Joy

Day 66

JUMPING ON A TRAMPOLINE, walking on a gymnastic beam, or riding a bike—all of these have something in common. In order to do these activities safely you need to be balanced and in alignment as a whole, otherwise you fall flat on your face while jumping and can't stay up on that beam, let alone bike safely.

Life is an aligned balancing act my dear aligner, expander, and calibrator; how will you practice to get better at it?

Align, Expand, and Calibrate - Your Stairway to Joy

Day 67

WALKING aligns you immediately because you are moving straight ahead—and mind you, that's without consciously thinking about it. Wow! Yes, you could also walk backwards, you silly you, but those steps are still in alignment and this time with extra connection since there is loads of play and laughter in such a fun activity—walking in a zig-zag, still aligned even in that fun pattern, maybe even more so.

You walk all day long, so tune into that always present alignment by becoming a conscious walker—breathe into that, jot down some zig-zag, straight, or curvy alignment walks!

Align, Expand, and Calibrate - Your Stairway to Joy

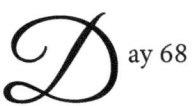 ay 68

LET'S stay with your walking for a bit longer…

Yesterday you were made aware of consciously breathing into an automatic alignment while walking. Today, let's practice expanding in that easily available alignment by imagining your energy becoming more humongous with every step—like being your aligned hugeness, trotting along your journey. How does that feel?

Align, Expand, and Calibrate - Your Stairway to Joy

 Day 69

Yes, we are still walking, aligning, and expanding—but today we take it even further by calibrating in this normal everyday activity. Are you ready?

An aligned, expanded, and calibrated being takes every step in pride, with the heart carried high and outward, shoulders broad and wide, a relaxed neck raising the head as high as it goes, eyes focused and filled with joy, lips cracked into a smile—all while being filled with inspiration, beauty, zest, wonder, awe, and phenomenal expectations on the mind.

That IS you—I know it! How do you feel, being exactly that?

_____
_____
_____
_____
_____
_____
_____
_____
_____
_____
_____
_____
_____
_____
_____
_____
_____
_____

Align, Expand, and Calibrate - Your Stairway to Joy

 Day 70

When you sit in a car at a red light and look into the side mirror you see a line of cars behind you—all neatly in line following the markings, signs, and stoplight. That right there is alignment—not to mention the honking noise-mess that would follow if even one of them would be out of alignment.

Your inner being is this alignment, your feelings are these signs - hence, when aligned you feel amazing and when not, you don't - and your body's physical symptoms are the noise of you being out of alignment.

You really have it all mapped out perfectly for you to align and know when you are dis-aligned. Do you see the magic in that?

Align, Expand, and Calibrate - Your Stairway to Joy

Day 71

WHAT KIND of day do you want, and how can you pair your clothing to match such a chosen new day—in other words, what aligned garments will you wear today? How will you feel in your magical attire? Why did you choose these articles and what are your expectations by wearing them? How can you expand in this perfectness and how will you calibrate in these fitting fabrics?

Align, Expand, and Calibrate - Your Stairway to Joy

 Day 72

BEING DIS-ALIGNED FEELS UNWELL SO, naturally, being aligned feels ecstatic—while somewhat aligned is anywhere in-between that feeling department. Where do you measure on this scale of bliss, and what can you do to heighten your spot?

Align, Expand, and Calibrate - Your Stairway to Joy

 ay 73

WHAT WOULD you tell a child that is not happy? How would you phrase your guidance to align, expand, and calibrate in a child-way? Would you use smooth, loving, kind, and playful words? Please, write them down.

Now, say these wonderful messages to yourself—in that same smooth and loving way. Why? Because you deserve to be kind to yourself, love yourself, and take gentle care of yourself.

Are you feeling your alignment, expansion, and calibration in this?

___

Align, Expand, and Calibrate - Your Stairway to Joy

Day 74

How many times are you with an open heart, giving, giving, and giving even more—just to close your heart again because of exhaustion, anger, or frustration, maybe even blaming this unwell shift on everyone else since they are needy or don't give much in return? Most would say "A lot!"

I have a wonderful solution for you: Be openhearted, make your well-feeling a priority, give only as much as you can, and stay openhearted. Smile! Then take care of yourself, give some more - stop giving when it's too much - and stay openhearted. Smile! And on and on you go…

That, my dear journaler is an aligned state in which you stay aligned, can expand, and will calibrate—all while sharing and spreading your incredible power. Well done!

_____
_____
_____
_____
_____
_____
_____
_____
_____
_____
_____
_____
_____
_____

Align, Expand, and Calibrate - Your Stairway to Joy

 ay 75

YOU ARE NEVER responsible for anyone else's life, you can never fix anyone or anyone else's life, and you can never live anyone else's life - kids, elderly, anyone needing your help, and common sense circumstances are of course excluded from the first two statements - however, you can support, help, and inspire, but only if you are aligned with who you really are.

How many people are you feeling responsible for? How many are you trying to fix? Are you trying to live for others? Are you serving others their life on a golden plate?

Stop that! Instead, use that energy to align, expand, and calibrate so you can shower your surroundings with what is really possible—your aligned inspirations, uplifts, and comfort, sprinkled with your expanded zest and calibrated jazz.

___
___
___
___
___
___
___
___
___
___
___
___
___
___

Align, Expand, and Calibrate - Your Stairway to Joy

 ay 76

WHEN OTHERS TELL you that something is not right for you, good for you, or talk against your choices and what's going on for you, ask yourself where they are coming from. Are they, as themselves, in an aligned state—or are they unaligned?

Most likely they are not aligned, because aligned people usually don't have the need to tell others how wrong something is since they normally see everything and everyone in their finest light, most positive life, and capable to handle their journey.

Are you listening to many of those unaligned beings? How can you put a stop to that? You guessed it—by aligning, expanding, and calibrating as your true YOU! Bravo!

Align, Expand, and Calibrate - Your Stairway to Joy

 Day 77

WHAT'S NOT WORKING for you right now, and how is this happiness-disruption showing itself?

Is your car not starting? Pointing out that *you* are not starting —maybe not creating enough life-fuel?

Is your pipe broken—representing pressure and possible old and clogging gunk in your life?

Is the go-button for the wash cycle not starting, highlighting that you are pushing too hard for too long by living life forcefully versus in the flow?

What is the problem, what does it mean, and how can you take these signals to heart—to align, expand, and calibrate yourself more often?

_____
_____
_____
_____
_____
_____
_____
_____
_____
_____
_____
_____
_____
_____

Align, Expand, and Calibrate - Your Stairway to Joy

# Day 78

WHEN A HEALTH CRISIS STRIKES, you can either sit in stagnance and its sulk - with that shift to dis-alignement and stay unaligned - or you can acknowledge the feelings that you are experiencing by allowing them in freely, then accepting, respecting, appreciating, thanking and loving them. From that state of peace of mind, body, and soul, on you go; aligning with this situation, expanding in the good of it, and calibrating into a higher YOU.

Because after all, every happening always has gold for you. Find that gold!

Align, Expand, and Calibrate - Your Stairway to Joy

Day 79

LIVING in paradise - a beautiful place in your eyes - makes it easy to align and also stay aligned; whereas living in an environment where views are not of that kind takes a bit more work—indeed, a great focus-practice to live on the bright side. That counts for wonderful situations versus hard life-events, no-drama versus drama-overload, and good times versus bad times.

But here's the thing: diamonds are created under pressure!

It boils down to how you can - and will - focus on aligning, expanding, and calibrating towards well-feeling when the opposite is more present—because the glorious is always available, even if microscopic.

How will you align with that one colorful flower in a shabby meadow? How will you expand in the sparkle of the heavy rain? How will you calibrate above the darkness?

Align, Expand, and Calibrate - Your Stairway to Joy

 Day 80

WHAT IN YOUR outer world makes you feel happy, fulfilled, over-the-moon alive, and like smiling without ever stopping? Make your joy-list, keep adding on, and go do those exact ecstasy actions more often! It's called perfect alignment—with the world, life, being here, and who you really are. Well done, amazing align-er!

Align, Expand, and Calibrate - Your Stairway to Joy

Day 81

Do you love sliding into a fresh new bed—getting between clean and amazing smelling sheets that are soft, yet starchy? Do you love putting your head on a freshly washed pillow case while hugging that clean piece of fluff lovingly? I certainly do!

Notice your automatic alignment with well-feeling, comfort, and an opening of your heart but also your expansion, by stretching your body left and right and moving your feet around with joy, and your calibration into the essence of *that's living*. It's wonderful and luxurious! Do you feel that shift?

Align, Expand, and Calibrate - Your Stairway to Joy

 Day 82

WHEN HUNGRY, eating is in alignment—and through the satisfaction of soothing your tummy, expansion into coziness is automatic and calibration from this nourishment is a given.

If tired, taking a nap will replenish you and is a healthy alignment—one in which you can restfully expand and calibrate to a peaceful you.

If sick, taking excellent care of yourself is the called for alignment, expansion, and calibration that gets you into a healing frequency.

You see, your physical needs always have your back. So how will you follow them without question more often?

Align, Expand, and Calibrate - Your Stairway to Joy

 Day 83

It's natural to now and then get caught up in anxiety, unsureness, or feeling frantic—after all, you are here for a lifetime. It's like going on a road trip and at some point feeling some sort of stress because it's a long drive. Question is, what do you make of it?

Asking yourself when these feelings are coming up if they are present time or back-in-time emotions and clearly listening to your inner answers will help you out; because digging deep into something that is not even real anymore - many times they are stemming from the ancient - never helped anything. For those antiques, choose to laugh them off as old gunk and shift your focus to having fun instead—for all others, breathe and know that they are normal.

Make your ancient-versus-actual list, then enjoy the alignment that's created. You so got this!

Align, Expand, and Calibrate - Your Stairway to Joy

 ay 84

I can't, I won't, I don't want to—no!

These expressions are usually thought of negatively or that the person using them is a bad human being. That's such an untruth! They are important to use as needed in order to align with what's right for you, and to not over-give or over-empty yourself at a constant rate.

When someone asks you for something, check in with yourself first—see if your tank of alignment, expansion and calibration is full. If it's filled to the brim, give and give, because it will be a joy. If empty or barely full say "Not now!" and fill yourself first, then give and give—again, what a joy.

This plan of action does not mean you don't help. On the contrary, you support from the best you-version that you can be, which is the only real and pure way to aid. Way to go, taking such wonderful care of yourself!

Align, Expand, and Calibrate - Your Stairway to Joy

 Day 85

ARE YOU LIFE-TIRED? Of course, at some point feelings of that sort are caught in everyone's life-nets. No biggie! But there is truthful understanding in these exhausted moments that you can use to supercharge yourself, by using these lower times to your advantage—which is what you came here to do and grow through to become wiser as you live.

So are you OK with how things are right now, or are you disaligned with the present; not expanded in what is going on, and not calibrating yourself in the given situation?

The latter is what is zapping your energy, not life or what's happening—it's your fight against physicality and a refusal to be OK with how it is.

However, that space of allowance for what IS to BE is exactly where all gold lies, because in that essence of being open to the unknown, aligned new solutions and fluent love for life exists. This is even true at the final stages of life.

What do you say, can you give yourself permission to align with how it is, expand with what is, and calibrate to a higher and wiser you in what IS—no matter what?

_____
_____
_____
_____
_____
_____
_____
_____

Align, Expand, and Calibrate - Your Stairway to Joy

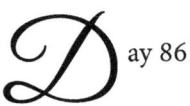ay 86

THE FREQUENCY OF ALIGNMENT, expansion, and calibration is one of limitlessness and wonders; meaning, that what you wish for is there too, since your desires are made of well-feeling and joy.

How can you get your bottom into that frequency more often?

Following your heart is definitely the way since your heart hosts your soul and produces your most powerful energy, which is your love—but what other ways are there for you to move yourself into bliss?

Align, Expand, and Calibrate - Your Stairway to Joy

Day 87

THINK OF A LITTLE CHILD—THE sparks in the eyes and the playfulness in the mind, but also always looking out for themselves, and with a natural - not thinking about it for a second - expectation that everyone follows them around, and that they are taken care of. Your inner you is like that—sparkly and full of light, playful indeed, with the expectation that you follow its lead unquestionably, take its wisdom to heart, and take care of yourself by aligning, expanding, and calibrating as it guides you to do. Are you willing to act on that?

___
___
___
___
___
___
___
___
___
___
___
___
___
___
___
___
___
___

Align, Expand, and Calibrate - Your Stairway to Joy

 Day 88

DID you ever pair a certain cheese with the perfect bread, an appetizer with the fitting main course, a drink to the right food?

How did you feel while doing so—did you research what would be best or go with what your gut said? Was there excitement, pride, and a deep knowing in that activity? I bet so because naturally alignment was created and you, consciously or not, latched onto that goodness and expanded and calibrated in it—hence, you felt amazing.

How can and will you do exactly that in every aspect of your life?

_____
_____
_____
_____
_____
_____
_____
_____
_____
_____
_____
_____
_____
_____
_____
_____

Align, Expand, and Calibrate - Your Stairway to Joy

 Day 89

WISHFUL THINKING IS your best friend!

Choose your wishes, think and feel them vividly—then follow up with feeling the amazing outcome. Smile! Wow, do you sense your shift?

This practice is so simple, yet so aligned with what you want in life—experiencing joy, bliss, health, abundance, and happiness.

You create with what you think and how you feel—so create well!

Align, Expand, and Calibrate - Your Stairway to Joy

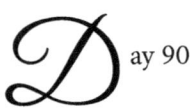 ay 90

So there is this thing you don't want to do—happens to the best of us!

Can you align with not doing it? Can you align with doing it anyways—but in a good fashion and a well-feeling essence?

There are only two good options—which one will it be?

Align, Expand, and Calibrate - Your Stairway to Joy

* * *

Ready to continue on your self-growth path? Get the next journal in this series: ***Magick and Broomsticks - The Portal to Your Wild Side***

BONUS

Because hey, no one ever wants the goodness to end.

Align, expand, and calibrate more and more— and onward you go!

# Day 91

HOW MANY TIMES will you infuse your personality, words, actions, and thoughts with your alignment, expansion, and calibration today? Or, at least, maybe I can get a potent "I'm giving my best to BE and live true to myself as much as possible!"

How committed are you—and can you commit even more?

Align, Expand, and Calibrate - Your Stairway to Joy

ay 92

BECOMING ONE with consciousness means that you become nothing—so you can BE nothing, think nothing, feel nothing, expect nothing, and do nothing in the space of this beautiful nothingness.

Try it! Close your eyes and lay your body flat—breathe yourself into being ONE with that pure and limitless emptiness that you are at your core. There, a deep relaxation can set in and everything you always wanted, asked about, came here to experience, and way more has a chance to BE because as and in that nothingness - which is actually an everythingness - you are stepping out of your own way and give the OK to openly allow and receive the unknown. How does that feel?

___

Align, Expand, and Calibrate - Your Stairway to Joy

 Day 93

BEING RADIANT, magnetized, vitalized, full of yourself, and in complete love with yourself - as well as thinking the highest of yourself - is healthy! It's called alignment, expansion, and calibration—it's your birthright to BE and live. What are you waiting for?

___

Align, Expand, and Calibrate - Your Stairway to Joy

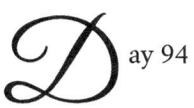 Day 94

TAKE your sweet time and practice becoming a genius *aligner*, *expander*, and *calibrater*! But beware, I did not say "stick your head into the sand until better times arrive." NOW is the only time that you have, so go for it spectacular *journaler*, you have my support—besides, you so got this!

Align, Expand, and Calibrate - Your Stairway to Joy

 Day 95

Nay-sayers, negative-ers, and down-ers are aligned, just not with what you are seeking to align with. Does that make it wrong? No! It just isn't what you want; hence, you are working with this journal. So with an I-dont-care-ness and I-let-them-be-ness, turn your head towards your heart to focus on your courtship with yourself—in which you love yourself enough to create alignment, expansion, and calibration as YOU.

Oh my, you are glowing! Must be your alignment!

Align, Expand, and Calibrate - Your Stairway to Joy

AND NOW IT'S YOUR TURN!

The following are your magical pages to align, expand, and calibrate in secret!

BE 100% true to yourself here!

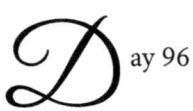 Day 96

I ALIGN, expand, and calibrate because…

___

Align, Expand, and Calibrate - Your Stairway to Joy

 Day 97

ALIGNMENT, expansion, and calibration gives me…

Align, Expand, and Calibrate - Your Stairway to Joy

 Day 98

Aligning, expanding, and calibrating makes me...

Align, Expand, and Calibrate - Your Stairway to Joy

Day 99

ALIGNMENT, expansion, and calibration creates…

Align, Expand, and Calibrate - Your Stairway to Joy

 ay 100

To ALIGN, expand, and calibrate is a creative lifestyle because…

___

Align, Expand, and Calibrate - Your Stairway to Joy

* * *

Don't forget to leave a review on Amazon.com and Goodreads.com as soon as you can, as your kind feedback helps other readers find my books easier. Thank you!

ALSO BY JACQUELINE PIRTLE

365 Days of Happiness

Because happiness is a piece of cake!

This passage book invites you to create a daily habit to live your every day joy, and is the parent companion to *365 Days of Happiness*, the journal workbook.

* * *

365 Days of Happiness - Special Edition

Because happiness is a piece of cake

This beautiful Special Edition of the bestseller *365 Days of Happiness: Because happiness is a piece of cake* has room for your notes after every daily passage.

* * *

365 Days of Happiness - Journal Workbook

Because happiness is a piece of cake

This enlightening journal workbook is your daily tool to create a habit of living your every day bliss, and is the companion to *365 Days of Happiness: Because happiness is a piece of cake*.

* * *

Life IS Beautiful - Here's to New Beginnings

If you like digging deeper into the meaning of life and are inspired by spirituality, then you'll love Jacqueline's effective teachings.

* * *

Parenting Through the Eyes of Lollipops

A Guide to Conscious Parenting

If you like harmony at home and laughter in the house, then you'll love Jacqueline's inspirational methods.

* * *

What it Means to BE a Woman

And Yes! Women do Poop!

If you like to live free, empowered, and want to decide for yourself, then you'll love Jacqueline's liberating ways.

* * *

Life-changing Journals

What. If. - Turning your IFs into it IS!

Open - Where it all starts!

To BE and Live - The reason you are here!

High for Life - The best case scenario!

Bragging - Because you're worth it!

Of Course - Because why wait...

Magick and Broomsticks - The Portal to Your Wild Side

Every journal comes in two lengths:

A 30 day journal

A 90 day journal - The Extended Edition

If you like being in charge of your own life, turning your dreams into reality, enjoy journaling, and want to squeeze the most out of your time, then you'll love Jacqueline's uplifting teachings.

ABOUT THE AUTHOR

Bestselling author, podcaster, and holistic practitioner, Jacqueline Pirtle, has twenty-four years of experience helping thousands of clients discover their own happiness. Jacqueline is the owner of **FreakyHealer** and has shared her solid teachings through her podcast **The Daily Freak**, sessions, workshops, presentations, and books with clients all over the world. She holds international degrees in holistic health and natural living. Her effective healing work has been featured in print and online magazines, podcasts, radio shows, on TV, and in the documentary *The Overly Emotional Child by Learning Success*, available on Amazon Prime.

For any questions you might have, to sign up for Jacqueline's newsletter, and for more information on whatever else she is up to, visit www.freakyhealer.com and her social media accounts @freakyhealer.

www.ingramcontent.com/pod-product-compliance
Lightning Source LLC
LaVergne TN
LVHW012114070526
838202LV00056B/5734